AND THEN MOSES WAS THERE

Voices from the Old Testament

Loretta Miles Tollefson

And Then Moses Was There © 2014, Loretta Miles Tollefson
Cover © 2014, Loretta Miles Tollefson

All Rights Reserved
LLT Press, Eagle Nest, New Mexico

ISBN- 0692209578
ISBN- 9780692209578 (LLT Press)

All Scripture quotations are from the King James Version of the Bible

Versions of the majority of these poems, as well as the Preface, were published in *Journey of the Shunammite* by Loretta Miles Tollefson, ©2003

This book is also available in e-book format at
www.lorettamilestollefson.com

PREFACE

No matter whether you believe the events in the Bible really happened or are "just stories," the people in those stories have much to teach us. It's easy to fall into the trap of thinking that the Bible stories aren't relevant to us today, either because we believe that the events they tell about didn't really happen or because they seem to tell us about people who had a special "in" with the Divine.

But we've all read at least one great novel or short story that helped us understand ourselves by pointing out the similarities between human beings that transcend culture and time. In the same way, the Bible stories can increase our understanding of ourselves and others. After reading these stories we can comprehend a little more clearly how even the wisest of men can justify actions of great folly. We can see why the seemingly simplest of girls can be called to enormous tasks, or what would compel a daughter-in-law to sacrifice everything to follow an old and poor woman into a land full of strangers.

And we can also see that these are men and women with human failings and strengths. They are not superhuman and thus able to experience God in a way we cannot. Nor are they less than human and in need of more-than-ordinary divine intervention. They are like us, and their link with the Divine is the same link we also can have. If they could, we can.

In the poems in this collection and in *Mary At the Cross* I seek to ask what might it have been like to be a particular individual in a specific Bible story. How might it have felt to live those circumstances? Why might that person have reacted in that way? There are no definitive answers to these questions. Like all great literature, the stories give us clues, but not answers. Those clues provide us with a springboard for meditating on the human emotions and reactions that bridge centuries and particular habits of life, as well as on Divine grace and love, which are not bound by space and time.

The poems in this book are the result of my own meditation and research. I hope they will provide a point of departure for you, the reader, as you also "think on these things."

Loretta Miles Tollefson, Feb. 2014

AND THEN MOSES WAS THERE

Voices from the Old Testament

Loretta Miles Tollefson

Contents

EVE 1
NOAH 3
TOWER OF BABEL 5
HAGAR 7
LOT'S WIFE 9
ABRAHAM 11
JACOB 13
PHAROAH 15
MOSES 19
RAHAB 22
CANAANITE SOLDIER 24
BARAK 27
GIDEON 29
JEPHTHAH AND HIS DAUGHTER 31
RUTH AND NAOMI 34
ELI 38
JONATHON 40
MEPHIBOSHETH'S SON 42
SOLOMON 44
JEROBOAM 46
JEZEBEL 49
ELIJAH 51
SHUNAMMITE WOMAN 54
ISRAELITE CHILD 57
HEZEKIAH 59
PROPHET 61
JEREMIAH 63
HOSEA 65

EVE

And the LORD God commanded the man, saying, Of every tree of the garden thou mayest freely eat: But of the tree of the knowledge of good and evil, thou shalt not eat of it: for in the day that thou eatest thereof thou shalt surely die. (Genesis 2:16-17)

And the serpent said unto the woman, Ye shall not surely die: . . . your eyes shall be opened, and ye shall be as gods, knowing good and evil. And . . . she took of the fruit thereof, and did eat, and gave also unto her husband with her; and he did eat . . . [Therefore] Unto the woman [God] said, . . . in sorrow thou shalt bring forth children. (Genesis 3:4-16)

Eve

They call it the fall.

As if life's fragments
can be caught up in
a package of words
and disposed of. What
the serpent didn't
say was that being
like God was not a good thing.
Possibility
eats at my heart,
insatiable worm.

Serpent of knowledge
slipping through the tall
grass, do not think
you deceive me now.
Now I see clearly

the danger you held.
The thoughts prick my sleep.
I watch my children
and wonder what lies
before us. What kind
of life will they lead?
How happy, how brave
in confronting life's scattered
pieces? And what more for them
then?

They call it the fall.

NOAH

And Noah went in, and his sons, and his wife, and his sons' wives with him, into the ark, because of the waters of the flood . . . They, and every beast after his kind, and all the cattle after their kind, and every creeping thing that creepeth upon the earth after his kind, and every fowl after his kind, every bird of every sort . . . And the waters prevailed upon the earth an hundred and fifty days. (Genesis 7:24)

Noah

>The waves sway
>the boat, a giant
>cradle. I cannot sleep.
>Collections
>of animals are built up
>with long treks through
>unknown lands;
>wood must be coaxed
>to fit a boat's contours,
>the pitch heated.
>There was no time then
>for staring into
>empty night.
>The beasts
>once they are fed
>are content. I toss
>on my thin bunk
>and stare
>into the black hold.
>The rain has stopped.
>The sun and the moon rise
>once again. My heart
>is glad, but still
>the gray waves sway the boat.

Water lies
in all directions. All
that is left
is to wait with
unsleeping eyes
in the darkness.

TOWER OF BABEL

And the whole earth was of one language, and of one speech . . . And they said, Go to, let us build us a city and a tower, whose top may reach unto heaven; and let us make us a name, . . . So the Lord scattered them abroad from thence upon the face of all the earth: and they left off to build the city. (Genesis 11:1-8)

The Tower

We thought we were of a piece,
made from the same dirt
colored brick, each understanding
all the others had to say.
When we agreed
to build the tall tower it seemed
a symbol of strength, tribute
to likemindedness.
How wrong we were we saw
as it grew. The cracks spread
through the walls deep
as canyons between us. Those
with brushes could not blend with
the carved work
of the others.
There were those with only
time to give and those who
offered money and orders. The cracks
deepened if we tried to shut
our eyes. In the end
we found we had tongues
we did not know, words
that had ached for growth
in a parched land. When we spoke

Loretta Miles Tollefson

our lips acknowledged
what our hearts had refused. Cracks
rumbled as they spread. Walls
crashed to the dirt they
had grown from and once
again we began
the long search for home.

HAGAR

And Sarai Abram's wife took Hagar her maid the Egyptian, . . . and gave her to her husband Abram to be his wife . . . and she conceived . . . And when Sarai dealt hardly with her, she fled from her face . . . And the angel of the Lord said unto her, Return to thy mistress, and submit thyself under her hands. (Genesis 16:3-9)

For Sarah conceived, and bare Abraham a son in his old age, . . . Wherefore she said unto Abraham, Cast out this bondwoman and her son: for the son of this bondwoman shall not be heir with my son . . . And Abraham rose up early in the morning, and took bread, and a bottle of water, and gave it unto Hagar, putting it on her shoulder, and the child, and sent her away: and she departed, and wandered in the wilderness of Beer-sheba. And the water was spent in the bottle, and she cast the child under one of the shrubs. And she went, and sat her down over against him a good way off, as it were a bowshot: for she said, Let me not see the death of the child . . . and the angel of God called to Hagar out of heaven . . . And God opened her eyes, and she saw a well of water; and she went, and filled the bottle with water, and gave the lad drink. And God was with the lad . . . (Genesis 21:2-20)

Hagar

It was not for her I returned
to bear my son on her knees.
I accepted my fate for the child's sake.
Always the handmaiden, never
to have the place of honor.
I cultivated gratefulness that he
might be recognized, a first born.
I could not conceive all her
bitterness. When her child was born, beyond
all expectation, her heart should
have exemplified grace. She

saw only a diminution of her
son's status. Against all reason,
custom, we must leave the camp.

Dry desert crusting beneath our
feet, the heat of an oven
in eddies around us. Such thirst. I thought
I had learned resignation but
to watch him die was more than
I was willing to bear. I still do not
know if the words rose from the heat
of my brain or the sudden
breeze that seemed to accompany them. All
I can say is that the water
I found saved us that day, gave
me strength.

I sit now on silken cushions
in the great tent beside my
strong son. His wives come to me with their small
problems. Oasis waters feed
our tall date trees. There is no
need now to cultivate gratefulness. Yet
the past remains what it is. I
will never forget.

LOT'S WIFE

And there came two angels to Sodom . . . and Lot seeing them rose up to meet them . . . And [they] said unto Lot, . . . the Lord hath sent us to destroy [this place] . . . and the [angels] laid hold upon his hand, and upon the hand of his wife, and upon the hand of his two daughters; the Lord being merciful unto him: and they brought him forth, and set him without the city . . . But his wife looked back from behind him, and she became a pillar of salt. (Genesis 19:1-26)

The Wife of Lot

There was much good in Sodom: Beauty
cool to the eye, green trees, pleasant paths,
smiling faces. The flowers bloomed always,
perfuming warm nights. Draperies fluttered
in morning sea breezes; bright ships brought
good things to eat and to wear. But in
the brightest of sun beams my husband
could see only dust. The beauty
of our bodies should be admired, not
shunted into dark holes. If the men
paraded, they had much to be proud
of, much to enjoy. What was it to me
what they did in the dark nights? When
my husband said we were going, I
thought he joked. Only when the youngest
of my sweet daughters was placed in his arms
did I follow. As we turned from
the gates toward those stark hills a shiver
ran through me. All dry trees and gray rocks.
Not even a shepherd's tent on the brown
grasses. It was natural enough that I look

back as we began the ascent. The salt
of my tears had already turned
my heart into stone.

ABRAHAM

And [God] said, Take now thy son, thine only son Isaac, whom thou lovest, and get thee into the land of Moriah; and offer him there for a burnt offering . . . And Abraham rose up early in the morning, . . . and went unto the place of which God had told him . . . And Isaac spake unto Abraham his father, and said, . . . Behold the fire and the wood: but where is the lamb for a burnt offering? And Abraham said, My son, God will provide himself a lamb for a burnt offering: so they went both of them together And Abraham lifted up his eyes, and looked, and behold behind him a ram caught in a thicket by his horns: and Abraham went and took the ram, and offered him up for a burnt offering in the stead of his son. (Genesis 22:1-13)

Abraham

>The boy came willingly enough. He
>had no reason not to trust me.
>At fourteen he did not chatter as
>he once had, but did bring to my
>attention an unusual flower,
>a particularly straight tree,
>the circling eagles. I acknowledged
>them all silently. I knew if
>I spoke my voice would betray me. I
>had not had the courage to tell
>his mother. He sauntered ahead of
>me overturning rocks to see
>the bugs scatter. I clucked at the ass
>with its load of wood and seemed not
>to hear the boy asking when we would
>be stopping for lunch. I had no
>appetite.

Loretta Miles Tollefson

We followed the trail up
the mountain. The rocks grew larger
and more plentiful. An eagle screamed.
I looked up at the sun and took
a deep breath, praying again for strength
to believe the impossible.
Again I felt that stillness deep in
my limbs, as if someone had placed
their hand on my shoulder. When he asked
me again when we would eat I
said there would be meat after we
sacrificed. I felt no surprise
that my voice did not tremble this time.

JACOB

And the Lord said unto [Rebekah], Two nations are in thy womb, . . . and the elder shall serve the younger . . . (Genesis 25:23-28)

[And Rebekah said unto Jacob] my son, obey my voice according to that which I command thee . . . And Jacob said unto his father, I am Esau thy firstborn; . . . arise, I pray thee, sit and eat of my venison, that thy soul may bless m . . . [Then Rebekah said unto Jacob] arise, flee thou to Laban my brother to Haran; . . . until thy brother's fury turn away; (Genesis 27:8-44)

And Jacob loved Rachel; and said [to Laban], I will serve thee seven years for Rachel thy younger daughter . . . And Jacob said unto Laban, Give me my wife, for my days are fulfilled, that I may go in unto her . . . And it came to pass, that in the morning, behold, it was Leah: and he said to Laban, What is this thou hast done unto me? did not I serve with thee for Rachel? . . . And Laban said . . . we will give thee [her] also for the service which thou shalt serve with me yet seven other years. (Genesis 29:18-26)

And when Rachel saw that she bare Jacob no children, Rachel envied her sister; and said unto Jacob, Give me children, or else I die. (Genesis 30:1)

And Jacob was left alone; and there wrestled a man with him until the breaking of the day. And when he saw that he prevailed not against him, he touched the hollow of his thigh; and the hollow of Jacob's thigh was out of joint...And Jacob called the name of the place Peniel: for I have seen God face to face, and my life is preserved. (Genesis 32:24-30)

Jacob's Nurse Deborah

> He was such a quiet boy.
> The large eyes watching, curls
> soft as smoke round his head,
> the sudden smile. He made
> old women feel tender.

His solemn words pleased his mother
as they talked by the hearth. She told
him then of the sayings,
though I begged her for silence. Dust
is best left underfoot;
the eyes grow confused when
wind lifts it carelessly.
But she knew her husband's mind, like
strong flint. When she told her son what
must be done, he went willingly
enough, only afraid
to be caught.

When he returned after
those many years, bearing his wives
and his children, he was much changed.
They say his wives' father
is like a fox, weaving low through
the desert night, appearing when
you least expect him, changing his
coat often. They also said that
Jacob was blessed by an angel,
though only after a wrestling
to the rough ground. He walked
now with a soft limp, his
eyes ever wary. He had grown
great, his wives clung to him and his
children and herds were many.

His smile was gone also,
but his boyhood love of good words
remained to him. In the long days

before I died he sat often
beside my bed and remembered
his mother, her words, and her ways.
A thread of sorrow ran
through all that he said. This man with
his wide flocks, many sons,
and strange adventures seemed to wish
only one thing: That in the days
when he had possessed nothing, sure
patience had had her hard way.

Jacob to Rachel

Bitterness shadows your mind, a lion
stalking its prey. Shine the torch of our love
in that dark place in your heart. Let it burn
the acrid mists to clear day.

You cling to this pain like a child clutching
at a treasured toy. Come, cleanse your sore heart
of the wrong your sister has done you, bar
it from the door of our adamantine
love.

You wrap your anger tight as a cloak round
your heart, a shield against the vast danger
of softness, then pain. Let this black shroud fall
from your shoulders into my waiting hands.

I will give you sons more precious
than a thousand children. Stalwart
and golden trees that will gladden
your heart, brighten our days.

Turn to me, wife of my heart.
Turn to me.

PHAROAH

And thou [Moses] shalt say unto him, The Lord God of the Hebrews hath sent me unto thee, saying, Let my people go. (Exodus 7:16)

And Pharaoh's servants said unto him, How long shall this man be a snare unto us? let the men go, that they may serve the Lord their God: knowest thou not yet that Egypt is destroyed? (Exodus 10:7)

Pharaoh

They say one of them was once
great in the land. They
are as dust now. I
and my fathers before me
have made them so.

They say their god has told
them to go and to worship.
After so many years they
still care nothing
for our gold-plated monuments, our largesse.

We wouldn't see their
tattered sandals again: jackals
and spotted hyenas would tighten
a fanged circle while vultures
drifted above on hot winds.

Why should he who holds
Egypt's scepter be brought
to heel by ragged slaves? Boils
and hail, darkness
like a blanket of cotton

smothering the face. What
more can they do? What tricks
can their faceless god
still hold in those
invisible sleeves?

Even my learned ones say
they must leave. They forget: I
am Pharaoh. To me only
are the godly powers
ascribed. The lack

of flies, the light
in Goshen mean nothing. If my
smooth headed men were
assiduous in their art
as in their words

the blood and the flies
would be as the other
tricks, foolish as they
would like me to seem. I
remain Pharaoh.

Upper and Lower Egypt live
in me. These impoverished
creatures forget themselves.
Only the hand of the Lord
of the Nile

can stay or release them.

MOSES

And the Lord said unto Moses, Come up to me into the mount, and be there: and I will give thee tables of stone, and a law, and commandments which I have written; (Exodus 24:12-18)

And when the people saw that Moses delayed to come down out of the mount, the people . . . said unto [Aaron], Up, make us gods, which shall go before us; for as for this Moses, the man that brought us up out of the land of Egypt, we wot not what is become of him . . . And all the people brake off the golden earrings which were in their ears, and brought them unto Aaron. And he . . . made it a molten calf: . . . And they rose up early on the morrow, and offered burnt offerings, and brought peace offerings; and the people sat down to eat and to drink, and rose up to play. (Exodus 32:1-6)

No Leader, No God

> It was at Sinai it
> happened. Moses, who had
> guided us out
> of mud bricked slavery
> went up into the rocks
> and didn't come back. We
> waited expectantly
> and then without
> expectation. Hope fades
> then and fear begins to
> seep into the cracks of
> your speech. You can't seem to
> look directly
> at one another. If
> Moses was gone, truly
> gone, where were we? Could we
> know how to turn with no
> leader, no god?

The braver among us
began to think what to
do, determined that a
god, at least, could be had.
For the moment
at least, we together
had the means to create
what we needed. The rings
and the necklaces, the
buckles, seemed small
on the wearers, but all
in a heap made enough
to plate a small standing
calf, hastily carved. Ah,
it was good to
have somewhere to look. The
calf glowed in the fire light.
We danced, happy to be
released from the gripping
uneasiness.
The mountain rumbled as
if in affirmation.
Aaron the priest raised his
arms to bless us, he said,
in our searching.
We stirred uneasily
and turned back to the fire.
The calf glowed more brightly
the faster we whirled. My
heart was joyful.
And then Moses was there.
His eyes blazed with anger.

His voice shook the black rocks.
As he faced us the dawn
began to grow
behind him. We watched the
calf lose its luster in
the cold morning light and
then we turned once again
to the mountain.

RAHAB

And Joshua . . . [sent] two men to spy secretly, saying, Go view the land, even Jericho. And they went, and came into an harlot's house, named Rahab, and lodged there . . . And the king of Jericho sent unto Rahab, saying, Bring forth the men that are come to thee, . . . And the woman took the two men, . . . and hid them with the stalks of flax, which she had laid in order upon the roof . . . Then she let them down by a cord through the window: for her house was upon the town wall . . . And [the Israelites] burnt the city with fire, and all that was therein . . . And Joshua saved Rahab the harlot alive, and her father's household, and all that she had. (Joshua 2:1-25)

Rahab

Those in the city's
high center see me only
as harlot.
In my father's house we have
always clung to each other. My
living has aided
those dearest to me and I
have learned much
from my dealings with both stranger
and friend:
the treasure of heart
and mind that the body
cannot feel, the way
a city crumbles
while appearing quite strong.
I see it all
clearly: once fragrant as flax
in bloom, as flax we are pulled
up by the roots, left
on the rooftops
to slowly rot. In due

time we will be crushed, our
walls broken.
Only the pliant
will be gathered
into the warp of life crouching
so patiently
out there on the plain.

CANAANITE SOLDIER

Wherefore Adoni-zedek king of Jerusalem sent unto Hoham king of Hebron, and unto Piram king of Jarmuth, and unto Japhia king of Lachish, and unto Debir king of Eglon, saying, Come up unto me, and help me, that we may smite Gibeon: for it hath made peace with Joshua and with the children of Israel . . . And it came to pass, . . . they were more which died with hailstones than they whom the children of Israel slew with the sword . . . And the sun stood still, and the moon stayed, until the people had avenged themselves . . . [Then Joshua] said unto the captains of the men of war which went with him, Come near, put your feet upon the necks of these kings . . . And afterward Joshua smote them, and slew them, and hanged them on five trees. (Joshua 10:3-26)

Without Mercy

When they say to fight,
I leave my fields
and go. It is not
for me to ask questions.

        I knew
there were strangers
in the land. The proudest
of our high hilled cities
had groveled before them.
They were like locusts,
the rumors said.
Taller than giants.

        I planted
my crops, tended
the single goat
and her hairy kid.
When I was told

to go, I kissed the baby, looked
into my wife's patient eyes,
trudged down the path.
The thick dust was warm
beneath my feet.

          My city
was one of five camped
on the plain. When
the enemy came
upon us we fought well, I thought. The battle
took the course of all such conflicts
until the hail began.

           Stones
the size of a man's fist
and as hard. To look up
was certain death.
The storm clung to us,
moved as we moved but did not extend
to the line where the enemy
stood. When the sun shone
once more, noon was long gone.

          They pressed
us again. Our kings
had long vanished
and we fought with dust
on our tongues. A sun without mercy,
no rest, no shadows
to hide in. More
spears coming through

the hot dust. They drove
us stumbling into
the caves on the dry hillsides,
across brown, treeless
plains to the narrow fences
of the few walls
remaining to us.

                    They tracked
us all, one by one.
Even our kings found
no mercy. We watched
the shadows stretch
out before these strange men
with their boots on our necks. Only
as our kings dangled, each
from his tree, did the darkness
descend.

BARAK

[And for] twenty years [Sisera] mightily oppressed the children of Israel. And Deborah, a prophetess, the wife of Lapidoth, she judged Israel at that time . . . And Deborah said unto Barak, Up; for this is the day in which the Lord hath delivered Sisera into thine hand: is not the Lord gone out before thee? So Barak went down from mount Tabor, and ten thousand men after him . . . Howbeit Sisera fled away on his feet to the tent of Jael the wife of Heber the Kenite . . . Then Jael Heber's wife took a nail of the tent, and took an hammer in her hand, and went softly unto him, and smote the nail into his temples, and fastened it into the ground: for he was fast asleep and weary. So he died. And, behold, as Barak pursued Sisera, Jael came out to meet him, and said unto him, Come, and I will shew thee the man whom thou seekest. (Judges 4:1-22)

Barak's Regrets

Everywhere the enemy had strangled
our land. No trade
for goods, rare the traveler
with news. The wall
of Sisera's chariots seemed
to block the very sun.

We did our best to take
pleasure in the small
things of life. Never looking
toward the horizon, keeping
our heads down.
Little we knew: in the end, the small
things would save us.

We could see
that Deborah was more
than just a mother

in Israel. We treasured
the words spoken beneath
her tall palms.
Still she was but
a woman,
no leader of men.

And Jael,
wife to a dweller
in tents, a man
friendly to his own
enemies. Small tool indeed
in Jehovah's great hands.
Mundane as a tent peg,
a workman's rough
mallet, or the soft banks
of an overfull brook.

To Deborah go the songs
of praise, to Jael the grim
satisfaction.
I, on the other hand, must
acknowledge God's
ways in it all.

GIDEON

And . . . the Midianites came up, and the Amalekites, and the children of the east, . . . and left no sustenance for Israel, . . . for both they and their camels were without number: and they entered into the land to destroy it . . . [And] Gideon threshed wheat by the winepress, to hide it from the Midianites. And the angel of the LORD appeared unto him, and said unto him, . . . Go in this thy might, and thou shalt save Israel from the hand of the Midianites: . . . Then the angel of the Lord put forth the end of the staff that was in his hand, and touched the flesh and the unleavened cakes; and there rose up fire out of the rock, and consumed the flesh and the unleavened cakes. Then the angel of the Lord departed out of his sight . . . And [Gideon] sent messengers throughout [all the land] and they came up to meet them. And Gideon said unto God, . . . Behold, I will put a fleece of wool in the floor; and if the dew be on the fleece only, and it be dry upon all the earth beside, then shall I know that thou wilt save Israel by mine hand, as thou hast said. And it was so: . . . And Gideon said unto God, Let not thine anger be hot against me, . . . let it now be dry only upon the fleece, and upon all the ground let there be dew. (Judges 6:3-39)

Gideon

>The swirling nomads were blinding
>as a desert storm, locusts
>eating the very
>leaves from our vines. We could
>only crouch helplessly
>in the hot hillside caves and close
>our eyes.
>
>I had dreamed so often
>of vengeance. Gideon
>the warrior, hewer

of far more than wood. Speaker
of truth, leader
of strong arms.

But I beat only grain and that hidden
on the floor of the wine press
for fear of the long legged camels.
Was this urge for the sword mine
or God's? Or only
a child's fantasy to be put away
with my sisters' dolls?

The angel and his fire had seemed
real enough. The armies of Israel had rallied
to my passionate
call. But the battle
was not yet waged. The fleeces
lay waiting at the mouth of the cave.

In the moment of transport
it is easy to believe, a great
comfort to speak.
In the cold light
of a damp dawn, reason
returns. That is when
I need the portents that even
others can see
to give steady shape
to my dreams.

JEPHTHAH AND HIS DAUGHTER

Now Jephthah the Gileadite was a mighty man of valour, and he was the son of an harlot . . . And Gilead's wife bare him sons; and his wife's sons grew up, and they thrust out Jephthah, and said unto him, Thou shalt not inherit in our father's house; for thou art the son of a strange woman . . . [But] when the children of Ammon made war against Israel, the elders of Gilead went to fetch Jephthah . . . and the people made him head and captain over them: and Jephthah uttered all his words before the Lord in Mizpeh . . . And Jephthah vowed a vow unto the Lord, and said, If thou shalt without fail deliver the children of Ammon into mine hands, Then it shall be, that whatsoever cometh forth of the doors of my house to meet me, when I return in peace . . . shall surely be the Lord's, and I will offer it up for a burnt offering . . . And Jephthah came to Mizpeh unto his house, and, behold, his daughter came out to meet him with timbrels and with dances: and she was his only child; . . . And she said unto her father, Let this thing be done for me: let me alone two months, that I may go up and down upon the mountains, and bewail my virginity, . . . And it came to pass at the end of two months, that she returned unto her father, who did with her according to his vow which he had vowed: and she knew no man. And it was a custom in Israel, That the daughters of Israel went yearly to lament the daughter of Jephthah the Gileadite. (Judges 11:1-40)

Jephthah and His Daughter

I was the only son of my mother,
hated for her sake,
denied my small inheritance
because of the gifts she received.

My father bore his scars deeply.
There was no need to ask how much
 he loved me, though I was only a girl.

When my brothers couldn't beat back
the long knifed marauders, they came to me.
I, whom they had pushed away
from their well-hung doors.

*He stood so proudly that day, the light
on his hair, eyes slitted
against the grit-covered wind.*

I came to Mizpah in triumph and in strength
I built the thick walls
and broad hearth of our home.
A house fit for the most honored of families.

*We had all that was necessary in Mizpah.
I, others to make music with, he the joy
of a man born to lead.*

In my tall strength I could see only
myself and my god. Yet even
a bargain made rashly must still be kept.
The law is hard as bricks, darkening the sky.

*I could not see him disgraced. He would
not be my father, if he were not proud. The weeks
I spent wandering were not all in pain.*

How the daughters of Israel cry for my dancing one
as they pass by my empty door.
They go to the mountains to weep, but they cannot
bewail my proud oaths as much as I do.

My father will love me always.
For his glory I gave myself to be sacrificed.
I will live in his dreams.

The dreams that were so strong within me
have died a natural death.
How can they live when there are no timbrels to play
warm songs beside my cold hearth?

RUTH AND NAOMI

... and the woman was left of her two sons and her husband ... Wherefore she went forth out of the place where she was, and her two daughters in law with her; and they went on the way to return unto the land of Judah ... And [Naomi] said, Behold, thy sister in law is gone back unto her people, and unto her gods: return thou after thy sister in law. And Ruth said, Intreat me not to leave thee, or to return from following after thee: for whither thou goest, I will go; and where thou lodgest, I will lodge: thy people shall be my people, and thy God my God. (Ruth 1:5-16)

[And Ruth] ... did according to all that her mother in law bade her. (Ruth 3:6)

So Boaz took Ruth, and she was his wife: ... And the women said unto Naomi, Blessed be the LORD, which hath not left thee this day without a kinsman. (Ruth 4:13)

Ruth

The old woman bade me
go. The caravan with
its safe passage
was waiting. She
would willingly see me
travel on her
Sabbath if it would find
me my people. I need
only walk through
the hut's door to return
to my parents, my friends,
the walls once so
familiar to me. I
gathered my possessions.
The ring he had
placed on my finger that

his parents had saved so
carefully for.
The sandals his father
had patiently knotted
with age gnarled hands.
The head scarf that mothering
love had made far softer than
mere cotton should
be. My sister-in-law
had tied her small bundle,
kissed the wrinkled
cheeks, stepped through the door. I
fumbled with the pots the
old woman had
helped me design. Somehow
the bundle was tied. I
stood in the door
looking at the hills. The
fields were heavy with grain.
My eyelids closed
against the bright sun. She
sat quietly on her
mat, watching me
with soft eyes. My leaving
would increase her
hardship but she only
bade me gently to go.
Dusk was falling
on the vine covered hills.
Her Sabbath had come. Still
she bade me go.
How many Sabbaths had

I helped her prepare for,
as a daughter
in the house? I found my
feet turning away from
the door. I placed
my bundle again on
its shelf and fumblingly
lighted the lamp.

Naomi

There are those who
say I had it all planned, a careful
diagram etched
into the hard packed floor
of our small hut, of my heart.
If only they knew.

The craving for justice for this
sweet, slim girl who had
followed me to a land
full of ways strange to her.
The knowledge
that there would be no reproach
if she spent all her years
sharing my pittance,
eking out the oil
of our lives.
The fear that my people's

traditions would be insufficient
to the need she didn't know she possessed.
How they haunted me.

There was no foreknowledge here, only
the urge to gently nudge
her forward, give counsel
I prayed would suffice, bow
my small frame before
the power that directed her steps.

ELI

Now Eli [the priest] was very old, and heard all that his sons did unto all Israel; and how they lay with the women that assembled at the door of the tabernacle of the congregation. (I Samuel 2:12-22)

. . . and [Eli's] eyes began to wax dim, that he could not see. (I Samuel 3:2)

[And] the elders of Israel said, Wherefore hath the Lord smitten us to day before the Philistines? Let us fetch the ark of the covenant of the Lord out of Shiloh unto us, that, when it cometh among us, it may save us out of the hand of our enemies. So the people sent to Shiloh, . . . and the two sons of Eli, Hophni and Phinehas, were there with the ark . . . Israel was smitten . . . And the ark of God was taken; and the two sons of Eli, Hophni and Phinehas, were slain. And there ran a man . . . to Shiloh the same day with his clothes rent, and with earth upon his head. And when he came, lo, Eli sat upon a seat by the wayside watching: for his heart trembled for the ark of God. (I Samuel 4:2-13)

Eli

They have taken the ark.
I, of all the people, know
how unclean are their hands
and my heart is heavy
as stone.
I sit as a stone, here
in my honored seat where
the city begins. I cannot
go in, though the shadows
show even my blind eyelids
that the day dims.
Eyes that could
do nothing but fall
before my sons' deeds.

How could I judge harshly
the work of my own hands?
I lived justly, took only
my portion, tried
to be fair. But they
lifted their heads from the cradle
with bold eyes, tore the toys
from their playmates' hands and laughed
when spoken to. I, judge
in Israel, head of the priests.
And now they have taken
the ark into a battle
no one has blessed.
God himself is taken
from us with unholy hands.
Within the walls my first
son's wife paces painfully, awaiting
my grandchild's birth, and I
sit here beside
the darkening road.

JONATHON

And Jonathan Saul's son arose, and went to David into the wood, and . . . said unto him, Fear not: for the hand of Saul my father shall not find thee; and thou shalt be king over Israel, and I shall be next unto thee; and that also Saul my father knoweth. (I Samuel 23:16-17)

And it came to pass on the morrow, when the Philistines came to strip the slain, that they found Saul and his three sons fallen in mount Gilboa. (I Samuel 31:8)

And the men of Judah came, and there they anointed David king over the house of Judah. (II Samuel 2:4)

Wherefore the Lord said unto Solomon, Forasmuch as this is done of thee, and thou hast not kept my covenant and my statutes, which I have commanded thee, I will surely rend the kingdom from thee, and will give it to thy servant. (I Kings 11:11)

Jonathon

I was prince in Israel, eldest
son of my
father's house. The doors
of the kingdom were open to me.
He, simple
shepherd, a boy sent
to serve brothers who laughed when he spoke.

My armor embossed by royal smiths.
His small sling.
We made a fine pair.
There was between us no need for words.
Our actions
corresponded each
to the other at play, in the field.

We could have ruled companionably
and well. He
leading us forward
with joyous fearlessness. I, the son
of courtly
life, looking always
behind with an eye to the future.

My father saw the man's strength, but not
his goodness.
The sword's edge was sharp,
the music not strong enough. In fear
of his crown
he cost me mine, cost
us all, with David's line, the kingdom.

MEPHIBOSHETH'S SON

Now when Mephibosheth, the son of Jonathan, the son of Saul, was come unto David, he fell on his face, and did reverence . . . And David said unto him, Fear not: for I will surely shew thee kindness for Jonathan thy father's sake, . . . and thou shalt eat bread at my table continually . . . And Mephibosheth had a young son, whose name was Micha. (II Samuel 9:6-12)

[And] David wrote a letter to Joab, . . . saying, Set ye Uriah in the forefront of the hottest battle, and retire ye from him, that he may be smitten, and die. (II Samuel 11:14-15)

. . . behold, Ziba the servant of Mephibosheth met him . . . And the king said, And where is thy master's son? And Ziba said unto the king, Behold, he abideth at Jerusalem: for he said, To day shall the house of Israel restore me the kingdom of my father. (II Samuel 16:1-3)

Mephibosheth's Son

My ancestors were mighty men.
My great grandfather stood taller
than all others
in the congregation.
My grandfather was straight
as the arrows that flew
from his tall bow. All
the stories say he was pure
as fine gold.

My father is a cripple. He crawls
to the usurper-king before
all the world.

They do not ask me
to pay homage. They think
me too young. But I am old
enough to know the value
of a seat at the king's table.
His bloody bread turns
to gravel on my lips. A man
who tricks his friends, who arranges
for his followers to die while
they fight his battles.

They think I am too young
to understand. But we
are of the tribe
of Benjamin. The blood
of warriors runs strong
in my veins. My time
will come. Saul's house
will rise again.

SOLOMON

And God gave Solomon wisdom and understanding exceeding much, and largeness of heart, even as the sand that is on the sea shore. (I Kings 4:29)

But king Solomon loved many strange women, together with the daughter of Pharaoh, women of the Moabites, Ammonites, Edomites, Zidonians, and Hittites . . . Then did Solomon build an high place for Chemosh, the abomination of Moab, in the hill that is before Jerusalem, and for Molech, the abomination of the children of Ammon. And likewise did he for all his strange wives, which burnt incense and sacrificed unto their gods. (I Kings 11:1-8)

Solomon

I prayed for understanding that night
in Gibeon. In the holiest
of our high places I asked the gift
to see beyond my people's eyes.
I wanted to rule them well.

My wives were many, emblems of wealth
who I came to love for their own sakes;
each marked by youth, her peoples' customs
and her own desires. I wanted
to know each one completely.

All the gods are alike in the end.
Molech Ammon's king, Jehovah our
mighty one. Hilltop altars of fruit,
our green booths at harvest. Each tells
the same story.

For my wives I built houses and for
their symbols, altars. Each also asked
 a small sacrifice, which I granted.
The totems we use give great comfort
to the heart in its need.

What could it hurt?

JEROBOAM

And [Ahijah] said to Jeroboam, . . . thus saith the Lord, the God of Israel, Behold, I will rend the kingdom out of the hand of Solomon, and will give ten tribes to thee.(I Kings 11:31-37)

[And they made Jeroboam] king over all Israel: there was none that followed the house of David, but the tribe of Judah only . . . Whereupon the king took counsel, and made two calves of gold, and said unto them, It is too much for you to go up to Jerusalem. (I Kings 12:20-29)

At that time Abijah the son of Jeroboam fell sick. And Jeroboam said to his wife, Arise, I pray thee, . . . and get thee to Shiloh: behold, there is Ahijah the prophet, which told me that I should be king over this people . . . he shall tell thee what shall become of the child . . . [And Ahijah said to her] Go, tell Jeroboam, Thus saith the Lord God of Israel . . . for thou hast gone and made thee other gods, and molten images, to provoke me to anger, and hast cast me behind thy back: Therefore, behold, I will bring evil upon the house of Jeroboam . . . and when thy feet enter into the city, the child shall die. (I Kings 14:1-12)

Jeroboam

The prophet had said I would know
when the time came.

I bade Israel to their
tents and the power ran
through my voice like lightning.
The obedience of men
is a strong wine.

We closed our borders
against Judah and knew
ourselves strong. But Jerusalem's
temple doors remained

open to tempt the unwary.
To choose between God
and king is a task for only
the most subtle of aged minds.

And so I bade statues
be built, one
for each border. Divine
symbols set up on hills
that were holy long
before David decided
to build God a house.
My voice was sure
and the people obeyed.

But now my lips can make
no sound.
The child who would have borne
the crown after me
lies dying. The prophet says
it is because I did not heed
God's voice, that the images
that bind the people to me will
be my dynasty's downfall.

There is nothing to be done.

And yet as I pace
my way through the long night
the questions rise
in me, unbidden. The small
whisper of conscience, the fire

in the bush, the urge
of mind or loins. Who
is to say what is God's voice
or man's heartbeat? To
turn back would have denied
the crown the prophet
had promised.

What else was I to do?

JEZEBEL

And [King Ahab] . . . took to wife Jezebel the daughter of Ethbaal king of the Zidonians, and went and served Baal, and worshipped him. (I Kings 16:31)

And Ahab told Jezebel all that Elijah had done, and withal how he had slain all the prophets with the sword. Then Jezebel sent a messenger unto Elijah, saying, So let the gods do to me, and more also, if I make not thy life as the life of one of them by to morrow about this time. (I Kings 19:1-2)

And of Jezebel also spake the Lord, saying, The dogs shall eat Jezebel by the wall of Jezreel. (I Kings 21:23)

And they went to bury her: but they found no more of her than the skull, and the feet, and the palms of her hands. (II Kings 9:35)

Jezebel

> My name is Jezebel. I am
> princess of Tyre.
> My ancestors lie
> in the carved rock.
> Baal and his consort Ashtoreth
> are my gods. We worship them
> on the hilltops, our sacrifices
> perfuming the air. We dance
> in celebration of his strength,
> her endless cycle.
> Our rituals were old before
> these shepherds entered our land.
> They did not adapt well
> to our ways. They held themselves
> aloof. Only the cultured
> among them admired
> our purple-robed women, our golden

artistry, the carved pillars
beside our altars. Many
of them are not so learned.
The prophet, for instance, thinks me
a symbol of wickedness.
I, his queen, child of rich Sidon. I
who kept my culture alive even
as his kind spread like flies
across our land.
I bow before the ancient names
and forms of male and female, rich
in image and ritual.
He has nothing
but a tribal god with no name,
a holy place no one may enter,
the emptiest of images.
His words hold no danger.
He is a pebble in my horse's
strong hooves, easily dislodged.

ELIJAH

And Elijah . . . said unto [King] Ahab, As the LORD God of Israel liveth, before whom I stand, there shall not be dew nor rain these years, but according to my word. And the word of the LORD came unto him, saying, . . . hide thyself by the brook Cherith, . . . And it shall be, that thou shalt drink of the brook; and I have commanded the ravens to feed thee there. (I Kings 17:1-4)

Then said Elijah unto the people, I, even I only, remain a prophet of the LORD; but Baal's prophets are four hundred and fifty men . . . let them choose one bullock for themselves, . . . and I will dress the other bullock, . . . and the God that answereth by fire, let him be God. And all the people answered and said, It is well spoken . . . Then the fire of the LORD fell, and consumed the burnt sacrifice, . . . [And]the heaven was black with clouds and wind, and there was a great rain . . . and [Elijah] girded up his loins, and ran before Ahab to the entrance of Jezreel. (I Kings 18:22-46)

[And Elijah] said, It is enough; now, O LORD, take away my life; for I am not better than my fathers. And . . . an angel touched him, and said unto him, Arise and eat . . . And he arose, and did eat and drink, and went in the strength of that meat forty days and forty nights unto Horeb the mount of God. I Kings 19:4-8

Elijah

> I know all the things
> He has done. The drought
> and the raven, circling black
> against the sun. The rind
> of bread brushed
> with grit where it fell
> beside the small brook.
>
> And strength to speak
> to a king whose face
> was darkened toward me.

The power welled up, a great
torrent. I spoke words
that brought prophets
of Baal to their trial. Even
the people of Israel
did as I said.

And then the rain.
Exultation of high wind. The king's
chariot was not as swift
as my feet.

My mind rehearses them all:
dreams half-remembered.

An angel has fed me a cake
baked on hot coals and provided
me water. My stomach
is full, the moisture not yet dry
on my lips, but I can see only
this tree and the harsh
blue of the sky
overhead.

It is all I can do to turn
my eyes to the path
leading south to Mount Horeb.
Moses saw a bush
burning there. There stone
yielded laws for all time. Perhaps

there I can find
once again the sound
of sheer silence
that my soul craves.

SHUNAMMITE WOMAN

And . . . Elisha passed to Shunem, where was a great woman; and . . . as oft as he passed by, he turned in thither to eat bread. And she said unto her husband, Behold now, I perceive that this is an holy man of God, which passeth by us continually. Let us make a little chamber, . . . and it shall be, when he cometh to us, that he shall turn in thither . . . And [Elisha] said, About this season, according to the time of life, thou shalt embrace a son. And she said, Nay, my lord, thou man of God, do not lie unto thine handmaid. And the woman conceived and bare a son . . . And when the child was grown, it fell on a day, that he went out to his father to the reapers. And he said unto his father, My head, my head. And he said to a lad, Carry him to his mother. And when he had taken him, and brought him to his mother, he sat on her knees till noon, and then died . . . Then she saddled an ass, . . . And when she came to the man of God . . . she said, Did I desire a son of my lord? did I not say, Do not deceive me? (II Kings 4:8-28)

Journey of the Shunammite

The praise of my village and friends,
the good works open to those
who are wealthy,
a man who treasured my steps.
My smile was calm, my heart silent. I did
not linger over
the babies placed in my arms
to be blessed.

The room for the prophet was another
good work. It pleased
me to provide for him.
There was nothing I asked in return, nothing
I needed.

And Then Moses Was There

When he spoke the impossible I willed
myself not to believe. My husband
was old, it was too late.
But hope plants a strong seed.
The very air became clearer,
the stars brighter. The song of the lark
as he flew caught
at my heart.

I had been told there
is pain when a child is born. I remember
only the wonder. From
his birth the chubby knees
were not still.
They became knobby and his shins dark
from the sun. Such sturdy shoulders
for a mere child. I combed
his curls with my fingers and he pulled
away with a laugh,
ran to play.

And now he lies silently
on the prophet's rough bed. His limp
body so cold against
the heat of the room. The blanket
scratched at my hands as I smoothed
down his clothes.

He is dead. I speak
to my heart as I did long ago, tell
it this is my lot.
Slowly I draw in my breath

and breathe out again. I pray
for acceptance but feel
only the salt of cold tears. Is this
my reward for honoring
a man with no home? To be twisted
with every emotion the wind
sends my way?

My mind had been calm
as the morning sky, silent
but gently glowing. A joy
I did not seek peered
through the slight clouds, erupted
into strong singing.
And now there is only
silence.
How can the memory of his laughter
be enough to ever balance
this pain?

ISRAELITE CHILD

For the children of Israel walked in all the sins of Jeroboam which he did; they departed not from them; Until the Lord removed Israel out of his sight, as he had said by all his servants the prophets. So was Israel carried away out of their own land to Assyria. (II Kings 17:22-23)

The Scattering

I was on the hill
behind the village
when they came: climbing
over the rocks, watching for snakes,
calling Miriam.
A full grown goat can
be a stubborn beast.
The rocks were hot and sharp beneath
my bare feet.

Children know much that
their parents never
say. We did not ask,
only huddled into corners,
comparing whispers.
Patchwork of horror
with no face. I had
climbed to the hill often, searching
for Miriam's good goat smell.

When I heard the screams
I dropped her head, dodging the rocks
as I ran for my mother.
But my father reached
me first. He caught me

by the arms and held
my face against his homespun chest.
I thought I heard her
screaming but there were
so many sounds. So
much fire. He could not have held me
too tightly.

She is not with us
now as they herd those
of us who are left
down the path like so many goats,
spears pricking our backs,
my father's hand tight
on my wrist.

We pass the green hill
with its great altar,
the tall stones with blank
faces. The village behind us
is silent.

The hills have turned rocky now.
My eyes search for gray,
sure-footed movement.
Miriam will be looking
for me. Her bags
will be heavy with milk.

HEZEKIAH

In those days was Hezekiah sick unto death . . . and he recovered . . . At that time Berodach-baladan, the son of Baladan, king of Babylon, sent letters and a present unto Hezekiah, for he had heard that Hezekiah had been sick. And Hezekiah hearkened onto them, and shewed them all the house of his precious things, the silver, and the gold, and the spices, and the precious ointment, and all the house of his armour, and all that was found in his treasures . . . And Isaiah said unto Hezekiah, . . . Behold, the days come, that all that is in thine house, and that which thy fathers have laid up in store unto this day, shall be carried into Babylon: nothing shall be left, saith the Lord. And of thy sons that shall issue from thee, which thou shalt beget, shall they take away; and they shall be eunuchs in the palace of the king of Babylon. Then said Hezekiah unto Isaiah, . . . Is it not good, if peace and truth be in my days? (II Kings 20:1-19)

King Hezekiah Restored

The smell of the sun on the flagstones
under my feet.
The look of the air swept
clean by the rain.
The leaves of the trees shiver
with light. Giddiness
of a new foal discovering its legs.

My heart continues to beat, my lungs
to expand. Each twitch
of my finger is a strange wonder.
Anything is possible and nothing
important but to drink
the renewed wine of my life.

The impulse of the moment is a glorious
thing, exaltation
of body and sense. The prophet
lectures at me about
something called consequences. Life
is too sweet to feel
sorrow for things that might
happen when I am gone.

Today I will walk my garden
path and cherish the hot sun
on my head. My only goal
is to continue
inhaling the scent of the flowers.

PROPHET

To what purpose is the multitude of your sacrifices unto me? saith the Lord: I am full of the burnt offerings of rams, and the fat of fed beasts; and I delight not in the blood of bullocks, or of lambs, or of he goats . . . incense is an abomination unto me; the new moons and sabbaths, the calling of assemblies, I cannot away with; it is iniquity, even the solemn meeting . . . Thy princes are rebellious, and companions of thieves: every one loveth gifts, and followeth after rewards: they judge not the fatherless, neither doth the cause of the widow come unto them. (Isaiah 1:11-23)

The Prophet

You speak of silk draperies
and God's glory.
A child with no coat slips through
stone streets. You lick
the crumbs of rich pastries from
your lips. A young
mother with thinning hair weighs
in her hands the one loaf which
must last the week.

You think it matters if you
pray in quiet
rooms or on sacred steps, your
beard is grown long
or cut in the new way. Men
are like dogs, they
will steal for lack of food and
you, as punishment, will make
them build temples.

But you. You will eat well this
night. You will lean
against soft cushions, sip your
foreign wines while
soft music plays, and speak in
puzzled tones of gaunt men who
rail on about some thing called
justice while your markets boom.

JEREMIAH

Now Pashur the son of Immer the priest, who was also chief governor in the house of the Lord, heard that Jeremiah prophesied these things. Then Pashur smote Jeremiah the prophet, and put him in the stocks that were in the high gate of Benjamin, which was by the house of the Lord . . . Then [Jeremiah] said, I will not make mention of him, nor speak any more in his name. But his word was in mine heart as a burning fire shut up in my bones, and I was weary with forbearing, and I could not stay. (Jeremiah 20:1-9)

Jeremiah

Why should I speak?
The words boil up
as in a covered pot.
No one hears.
They think me an old man with
a grudge against women
and wine. If there
is a God why should
he come to me only? They
laugh, or worse,
turn away.
I try to be still.
No one will listen
anyway.

Why should I speak?
Why give warnings
to a people who cannot hear?
I break pots,
no one sees.
I speak in the court
of the king himself, they

turn away.
I could go almost
naked and not an eye
would quiver.
I try to be still. No one
will listen
anyway.

Why should I speak?
The most apt of phrases
stick to me like burrs
on a mangy dog's coat.
Images crash
through my bones with
every step.
The multiplicity
of the words fills
my throat to choking.
The swirling thoughts must
spill from the dam
or drive me mad.
I try to be still. No one will
listen anyway.

HOSEA

Then said the Lord unto me, Go yet, love a woman beloved of her friend, yet an adulteress, according to the love of the Lord toward the children of Israel, who look to other gods, and love flagons of wine. So I bought her to me for fifteen pieces of silver, and for an homer of barley, and an half homer of barley: And I said unto her, Thou shalt abide for me many days; thou shalt not play the harlot, and thou shalt not be for another man: so will I also be for thee. (Hosea 3:1-3)

Hosea

She had eyes that seemed to look
into your soul while deflecting
your glance. Her young
body was slim, her face
unformed. I knew her
history but her image
would not leave my mind.

I married her in a hail
of holy oaths. How beautiful
she was that day. Our
love was strong. I was
a true husband to her.
Life was pleasant and children
were born to us.

I do not know when she began
to go again to the hilltops.
I watched for signs
that her heart had failed
toward me but her eyes
remained remote and clear. When
I woke in the night

her pillow was empty,
the children whimpering.
The names I had given them
described their own mother's
heart. When she left, all
the neighbors said
I was well rid of her.

But still I was haunted
by images. That soft face, those
relentless eyes. The dark
lips and the slender hands.
When word came, I went
gladly. I paid her debts while
the neighbors clucked.

We live now in a house
filled with veils. I speak
to her carefully in simple
words. I do not dare
tell her what lies
in my heart or ask
if she is free
to give me hers.

Is this what is meant when
they say that God despairs
over Israel? I try to forget
but those first nights cling

to me like the smell
of sweet oranges. The child
with his mother's great eyes follows
me everywhere.

www.ingramcontent.com/pod-product-compliance
Lightning Source LLC
Chambersburg PA
CBHW072106290426
44110CB00014B/1845